GALE
CENGAGE Learning

MW00469609

Nonfiction Classics for Students, Volume 1

Staff

Editor: Elizabeth Thomason.

Contributing Editors: Reginald Carlton, Anne Marie Hacht, Michael L. LaBlanc, Ira Mark Milne, Jennifer Smith.

Managing Editor, Literature Content: Dwayne D. Hayes.

Managing Editor, Literature Product: David Galens.

Publisher, Literature Product: Mark Scott.

Content Capture: Joyce Nakamura, *Managing Editor*. Sara Constantakis, *Editor*.

Research: Victoria B. Cariappa, *Research Manager*. Cheryl Warnock, *Research Specialist*. Tamara Nott, Tracie A. Richardson, *Research Associates*. Nicodemus Ford, Sarah Genik, Timothy Lehnerer, Ron Morelli, *Research Assistants*.

Permissions: Maria Franklin, *Permissions Manager.* Shalice Shah-Caldwell, *Permissions Associate.* Jacqueline Jones, *Permissions Assistant.*

Manufacturing: Mary Beth Trimper, *Manager, Composition and Electronic Prepress.* Evi Seoud, *Assistant Manager, Composition Purchasing and Electronic Prepress.* Stacy Melson, *Buyer.*

Imaging and Multimedia Content Team: Barbara Yarrow, *Manager.* Randy Bassett, *Imaging Supervisor.* Robert Duncan, Dan Newell, *Imaging Specialists.* Pamela A. Reed, *Imaging Coordinator.* Leitha Etheridge-Sims, Mary Grimes, David G. Oblender, *Image Catalogers.* Robyn V. Young, *Project Manager.* Dean Dauphinais, *Senior Image Editor.* Kelly A. Quin, *Image Editor.*

Product Design Team: Kenn Zorn, *Product Design Manager.* Pamela A. E. Galbreath, *Senior Art Director.* Michael Logusz, *Graphic Artist.*

Copyright © 2001

The Gale Group
27500 Drake Road
Farmington Hills, MI 48331-3535

ISBN 0-7876-5381-0
ISSN 1533-7561
Printed in the United States of America.

10 9 8 7 6 5 4 3 2 1

The Making of the Atomic Bomb

Richard Rhodes

1987

Introduction

The Making of the Atomic Bomb, by Richard Rhodes, was first published in 1987. For this detailed documentation of the development of the most destructive war weapon ever to be created, Rhodes received widespread recognition, winning the 1987 National Book Award, the 1988 Pulitzer Prize for General Nonfiction, and the 1988 National Book Critics Circle Award for General Nonfiction.

Rhodes provides extensive information on the biographical background and scientific accomplishments of the international collaboration of scientists that culminated in the creation of the first atomic bomb. In 1939, several scientists became aware of the theoretical possibility of creating an atomic bomb, a weapon of mass destruction vastly exceeding the potential of existing military arsenals. But it was not until the United States entered World War II, late in 1941, that priority was given to funding and organizing research into the creation of such a weapon in a secret operation referred to as the Manhattan Project.

The first test atomic bomb, called Trinity, was exploded in the New Mexico desert on July 16, 1945. On August 6, an atomic bomb was dropped on the Japanese city of Hiroshima. Three days later, another atomic bomb was dropped on the Japanese city of Nagasaki. On August 14, 1945, Japan agreed to an unconditional surrender to the Allies, thus ending World War II.

Rhodes addresses the difficult moral and ethical dilemmas faced by the scientists of the Manhattan Project, particularly the implications of creating such a weapon of mass destruction. Originally concerned with "pure" scientific research, those who worked on the Manhattan Project were forced to consider the ultimate effect of their research efforts on the future of the human race.

Richard Lee Rhodes was born in Kansas City, Kansas, on July 4, 1937, the son of Arthur Rhodes, a railroad mechanic and Georgia (maiden name Collier) Rhodes. When he was only thirteen months old, his mother committed suicide. Richard's eldest brother went to live with relatives while Richard and his brother, Stanley, who was two years older, stayed with their father. When Richard was ten, their father remarried, and their stepmother, Anne Ralena Martin, began a reign of terrifying physical and emotional abuse against the boys while their father passively looked on. After two years of deprivation, torture, and violence, Stanley sneaked out of the house to report this abuse to the police. The boys were removed from their home by state officials and placed in the Drumm Institute, a home for boys near Independence, Missouri. Although the Drumm Institute imposed strict rules upon the boys, who were also required to work at farming, Richard thrived in this environment, becoming an avid reader. In 1955, he graduated from high school with a scholarship to Yale University, in New Haven, Connecticut. He attended Yale from 1955 to 1959, graduating with a bachelor's degree in intellectual history.

Rhodes worked as a writer trainee for *Newsweek* magazine in 1959. In 1960, he married Linda Iredell Hampton and began working as a staff assistant for Radio Free Europe, in New York City.

Rhodes joined the Air Force Reserve from 1960 to 1965, during which time he worked as an instructor in English at Westminster College, in Fulton, Missouri, (from 1960 to 1961) and found work as an editor. Rhodes became book editing manager for Hallmark Cards in Kansas City, Missouri, from 1962 to 1970. He was a contributing editor to *Harper's* magazine from 1970 to 1974. He divorced Linda in 1974 and began working as a contributing editor for *Playboy* magazine in Chicago from 1974 to 1980. In 1976, he married Mary Magdalene Evans, whom he later divorced. Rhodes became a contributing editor for *Rolling Stone* magazine, in New York City, from 1988 to 1993. During this time, he was also a visiting fellow in the Defense and Arms Control Study Program at Massachusetts Institute of Technology (1988-1989), and a visiting scholar in the History of Science Department at Harvard University. Although Rhodes had been a severe alcoholic for thirty years, he was inspired to quit drinking by his love for Ginger Untrif, who became his third wife.

The Scientists

Rhodes describes extensively, up to World War II, the lives and work of an international community of scientists, mostly physicists and chemists, whose work eventually culminated in the making of the first atomic bomb. Theories of the existence of atomic particles date back to Greek philosophy in the fifth century B.C., and, by the seventeenth century A.D. most scientists assumed the existence of the atom. However, no actual proof of the existence of the atom had been formulated until J. J. Thomson discovered the electron in 1897. In 1884, Thomson was chair of the distinguished Cavendish Laboratory at Cambridge where he exerted tremendous influence on a generation of scientists. Einstein's revolutionary theory of relativity was announced in 1915. Leo Szilard, a Hungarian-born Jewish theoretical physicist, entered the University of Berlin in 1921, where he collaborated with Einstein. Ernest Rutherford was a New Zealand born British physicist credited with inventing nuclear physics (also called atomic physics). Rutherford studied under Thomson at the Cavendish Laboratory, replacing Thomson as head of the lab in 1919. Rutherford's most significant accomplishment was the development of a theory of atomic structure called the Rutherford atomic model.

Niels Bohr, a Danish physicist, made significant advances with his formulation of the Bohr atomic model. In 1921, Bohr became director of the Institute for Theoretical Physics in Copenhagen, which, under his direction, soon gained an international reputation as a leading center for research on quantum theory and atomic physics. Bohr broke new ground in the application of quantum theory to the study of atomic and molecular particles. Robert J. Oppenheimer, an American theoretical physicist, studied atomic physics under Rutherford at the Cavendish Laboratory. In 1927, Oppenheimer took a post in physics at The University of California at Berkeley and the California Institute of Technology. In 1932, James Chadwick, an English physicist who worked with Rutherford at the Cavendish Laboratory, discovered the neutron. Otto Hahn, a German chemist who was working with Fritz Strassmann, discovered nuclear fission. The Italian physicist Enrico Fermi conducted important research on nuclear fission at the University of Rome.

When Hitler came to power in Germany in 1933, many of Europe's greatest physicists emigrated in order to flee Nazi persecution, several of them settling in the United States. Szilard emigrated to London, where he first conceived of the possibility of creating an atomic bomb, and later settled in the United States, taking a post at Columbia University. Einstein, in particular danger of Nazi persecution due to his international prominence, fled to the United States, where he took a post at the Institute for Advanced Study at

Princeton University, in New Jersey. In 1938, Fermi, under the pretext of traveling with his family to Sweden to receive his Nobel Prize, fled fascist Italy, eventually settling in the United States. Meitner fled Nazi Germany in 1938 to settle in Sweden, where she continued her research with her nephew Otto Frisch. After Nazi Germany invaded Denmark, at the outbreak of World War II, Bohr and his family fled to England and then the United States.

The Manhattan Project

Upon reaching New York in 1939, Bohr alerted Einstein to the possibility of Germany developing an atomic bomb. Along with several colleagues, Bohr persuaded Einstein to write a letter to President Franklin D. Roosevelt, suggesting that the United States initiate research into the development of an atomic bomb before Germany developed one. However, government officials failed to comprehend the enormity of the implications of these new developments, as explained by several brilliant scientists. It was not until the bombing of Pearl Harbor in December of 1941 that the United States entered World War II, at which point the possibility of creating such a military weapon appeared more relevant to government and military officials. The result was the organization in May of 1942 of the secret Manhattan Project, which included several teams of American and British scientists conducting research at such disparate sites as the University of Chicago and Los Alamos, New Mexico. Other locations where scientists were working on the Manhattan Project were the University of California at Berkeley, Columbia University in New York City, and Oak Ridge in Tennessee. It came to be called the Manhattan Project because of the location of the new government office organizing the project, known as the Manhattan Engineer District Office. (The Los Alamos site, however, is most commonly associated with the Manhattan Project.) On July 16, 1945, the first test atomic bomb, named Trinity, was successfully exploded on an air base in Alamogordo, New Mexico. In the meantime, scientists in Great Britain, Germany, Japan, and Russia were coming to the same conclusions about the possibility of creating an atomic bomb. However, several factors discouraged efforts by these nations to develop such a bomb.

Hiroshima and Nagasaki

On April 12, 1945, President Roosevelt died, and Vice President Harry S. Truman was sworn in as president of the United States. Up to that point, Truman had only a vague idea of the goals of the Manhattan Project; he was quickly informed of the significance of its efforts. In May 1945, Germany surrendered to the Allies. Peace negotiations were initiated at the Potsdam Conference, held in a suburb of Berlin, from July 17 to August 2, 1945. President Truman of the United States, Prime Minister Winston Churchill of Great Britain, and Premier Joseph Stalin of Russia, known collectively as the Big Three, were the leading figures in these negotiations. The War with Germany concluded, the Allies sent a message from Potsdam to the Japanese government, calling for unconditional surrender. When Japan refused to surrender, the United States dropped the first offensive atomic bomb on the city of Hiroshima, Japan, on August 6, 1945. The bomb, nicknamed Little Boy, had been carried in a modified B-29 bomber called Enola Gay, flown by Colonel Paul Tibbets. Although the Japanese Emperor Hirohito was willing to surrender, the Japanese military was unyielding, as a result of which the United States dropped a second bomb, nicknamed Fat Man, on the city of Nagasaki, on August 9. Japan immediately surrendered to the Allies. Both Japanese cities were utterly devastated by the bombs. Hiroshima, with a population of about 350,000, suffered the deaths of 140,000 people as a result of the bombing. Two-thirds of the city was demolished in the explosion. Of Nagasaki's 270,000 residents, some 70,000 died as a result of the bombing, and half of the city was demolished. After the war, the United States began work on developing the more powerful hydrogen bomb.

Niels Bohr

Niels Bohr (1885-1962) was a Danish physicist known as the first to apply quantum theory to the study of atomic and molecular particles. He is also known for proposing the liquid model of the atomic nucleus and for formulating the Bohr theory of the atom. Bohr received a doctoral degree from the University of Copenhagen in 1911. He studied under J. J. Thomson at Cambridge University in England, but, when he learned that Thomson was not interested in his work, Bohr left to work under Ernest Rutherford in Manchester, England. There, Bohr distinguished himself by formulating the Bohr atomic model. He returned to Copenhagen in 1912 and in 1921 was named director of the Institute for Theoretical Physics. Under his direction, the Institute soon gained an international reputation for research in quantum theory and atomic physics. Bohr's principle of complementarity offered a theoretical basis for quantum physics, which became widely accepted among many scientists, although Albert Einstein continued to dispute it. Bohr's ground-breaking "liquid drop" model of the atomic nucleus and his "compound nucleus" model of the atom led other scientists to the discovery of nuclear fission. With the outbreak of World War II, Nazi Germany invaded Denmark, as a result of which Bohr and his family fled the country for

England and then the United States. He worked on the Manhattan Project in Los Alamos, New Mexico, which developed the first atomic bomb. However, Bohr expressed concern throughout his life about the threat to humanity posed by nuclear warfare.

Sir James Chadwick

James Chadwick (1891-1974) was an English physicist credited with the discovery of the neutron, for which he received a Nobel Prize in 1935. Chadwick worked with Ernest Rutherford at the Cavendish Laboratory in Cambridge, England, in researching properties of the atomic nucleus. In 1945, he received the honor of being knighted for his accomplishments.

Media Adaptations

- *The Making of the Atomic Bomb*, by Richard Rhodes, was recorded on audiocassette by Books on Tape in 1992.

Arthur Compton

Arthur Compton (1892-1962) was an American physicist who shared the Nobel Prize for Physics in 1927 for his research on X rays. Compton received his doctorate from Princeton University in 1916. In 1920, he was made head of the department of physics at Washington University in St. Louis, Missouri. Compton's research helped to make legitimate Einstein's quantum theory, which was not yet widely accepted among scientists. In 1923, Compton became professor of physics at the University of Chicago, a post that he retained until 1945. He became the chairman of the committee of the National Academy of Sciences that in 1941 conducted research into the potential development of nuclear weapons, ultimately organizing the Manhattan Project. Compton worked on the Manhattan Project as the director of the University of Chicago Metallurgical Laboratory from 1941 to 1945.

Albert Einstein

Albert Einstein (1879-1955) was a German-Jewish physicist whose theories of relativity forever changed scientific approaches to space, time, and gravity. Einstein was awarded the Nobel Prize for physics in 1921. After Hitler came to power in 1933, Einstein fled Nazi Germany, eventually taking a post at the Institute for Advanced Study at Princeton University in New Jersey, where he remained for the rest of his life. In 1939, Niels Bohr alerted Einstein to the possibility that Germany could develop an atomic bomb. Bohr asked Einstein to write a letter to President Franklin D. Roosevelt, suggesting that the United States initiate research on an atomic bomb. Einstein, however, was not involved in the research carried out by the Manhattan Project and was not even aware of the successful development of the atomic bomb until after it was dropped on Hiroshima. In the wake of this event, Einstein became a vocal advocate for world peace and the prevention of further nuclear warfare.

Enrico Fermi

Enrico Fermi (1901-1954) was an Italian-born physicist who won the Nobel Prize for physics in 1938 for his research on nuclear fission. Fermi earned a doctoral degree at the University of Pisa for his research on X rays. In 1926, he became a professor of theoretical physics at the University of Rome, where he was instrumental in developing a community of brilliant young physicists. On the pretext of traveling to Sweden to receive his Nobel Prize, Fermi fled fascist Italy with his family and settled in the United States. In New York City, Fermi met with other nuclear physicists, eventually becoming a part of the Manhattan Project. Based at the University of Chicago, he developed the first self-sustained nuclear chain reaction, which quickly lead to the making of the first atomic bomb. He became an American citizen in 1944 and, in 1946, was named professor of Nuclear Studies at the University of Chicago.

Richard Feynman

Richard Feynman (1918-1988) was an American theoretical physicist who received the Nobel Prize for physics in 1965 for his work on the theory of quantum electrodynamics. Feynman received his doctorate from Princeton University in 1942. From 1941 to 1942, he worked on the Manhattan Project in Princeton, joining the laboratory at Los Alamos, New Mexico, in 1943. Feynman was among the youngest scientists to hold a leadership position at Los Alamos. From 1945 to 1950, he worked as an associate professor at Cornell University, and from 1950 until his retirement he worked as a professor of theoretical physics at the California Institute of Technology. Feynman is considered one of the most brilliant scientific minds of the twentieth century.

Otto Frisch

Otto Frisch (1904-1979) was an Austrian-born physicist who worked on the Manhattan Project at Los Alamos, New Mexico. Frisch earned his doctorate degree at the University of Vienna in 1926. He worked with his aunt, the physicist Lise

Meitner, together discovering and naming uranium fission in 1939. After the War, Frisch became director of the nuclear physics department of the Cavendish Laboratory at Cambridge University in England.

Brigadier General Leslie R. Groves

In September 1942, Brigadier General Leslie R. Groves (1896-1970) was named head of the Manhattan Engineer District, in charge of all army activities concerned with the Manhattan Project. Groves was responsible for contracting independent building industries to construct the facilities at the various research and production sites that made up the Manhattan Project, such as a gaseous diffusion separation plant and a plutonium production facility.

Otto Hahn

Otto Hahn (1879-1968) was a German chemist who won the Nobel Prize for chemistry in 1944 for his discovery (along with Fritz Strassmann) of nuclear fission. Hahn received a doctorate degree from the University of Marburg in 1901. At the University of Berlin, he conducted research on radioactivity and in 1911 joined the Kaiser Wilhelm Institute for Chemistry. During World War I, he was instrumental in developing chemical warfare. Although his research was instrumental to the development of the atomic bomb, throughout the remainder of his life he opposed the further development of nuclear weapons.

Lise Meitner

Lise Meitner (1878-1968) was a Jewish Austrian-born physicist whose collaborative research with Otto Hahn, Fritz Strassmann, and her nephew Otto Frisch resulted in the discovery and naming of uranium fission. Meitner received her doctorate from the University of Vienna in 1906. In 1907, she began working with Hahn in Berlin on research in radioactivity. In 1938, she fled Nazi Germany for Sweden.

Robert Oppenheimer

Robert J. Oppenheimer (1904-1967) was an American theoretical physicist most widely known as the director of the Los Alamos laboratory of the Manhattan Project, which developed the first atomic bomb. Upon graduating from Harvard, Oppenheimer studied atomic physics under Lord Rutherford at the Cavendish Laboratory at Cambridge. He received his doctoral degree from Göttingen University in 1927, after which he taught physics at the University of California at Berkeley and the California Institute of Technology. His collaboration with a team of scientists on the Manhattan Project lead to the first nuclear explosion test in 1945 at Alamogordo, New Mexico. In 1947, Oppenheimer took a post as head of the Institute for Advanced Study at Princeton University. From 1947 to 1952, he was chairman of the General

Advisory Committee of the Atomic Energy Commission. In 1953, during the Red Scare in which many intellectuals were accused of treason, Oppenheimer was put on trial for suspicion of having leaked military secrets, based on his earlier sympathies with communism. He was found not guilty, but his position with the Atomic Energy Commission was terminated. The Federation of American Scientists, however, supported Oppenheimer. In 1963, President Lyndon B. Johnson presented Oppenheimer with the Enrico Fermi Award of the Atomic Energy Commission, thus officially retracting all public denunciation of the scientist.

Sir Rudolf Peierls

Rudolf Peierls (1907-1995) was a German-born physicist whose theoretical work was instrumental in the development of the atomic bomb. Peierls worked with Otto Frisch at the University of Birmingham, in England, where they collaborated on a memo explaining the theories that suggested the possibility of creating an atomic bomb. He became a British citizen in 1940 and in 1943 joined the team of British scientists who moved to Los Alamos, New Mexico, to work on the Manhattan Project. After the war, he returned to his post as a professor at Birmingham. In 1963, he left Birmingham to become a professor at the University of Oxford. Peierls was knighted in 1968.

Max Planck

Max Planck (1858-1947) was a German theoretical physicist who was awarded the 1918 Nobel Prize for physics for his formulation of quantum theory. Planck earned his doctoral degree in 1879 from the University of Munich. In 1892, he became a professor at the University of Berlin, a position that he held throughout his life. Although it was not immediately recognized as such by the scientific community, his quantum theory eventually revolutionized theoretical physics. While Einstein was instrumental in championing Planck's achievement, Planck was instrumental in calling attention to the significance of Einstein's theory of relativity. Although Planck was openly opposed to Hitler's racist policies, he remained in Germany throughout World War II to continue his research.

President Franklin Roosevelt

President Franklin Delano Roosevelt (1882-1945) was in his third term of presidency when the United States entered World War II. In 1939, he received a letter from Einstein alerting him to the potential for developing an atomic bomb, but he failed to see the true significance of this information until the United States entered the war in 1941. Roosevelt died in office on April 12, 1945, several months before the dropping of the first atomic bombs and ending of World War II.

Sir Ernest Rutherford

Ernest Rutherford (1871-1937) was a New Zealand-born British physicist awarded the Nobel Prize for chemistry in 1908 for his research that led to the development of nuclear physics (also referred to as atomic physics). In 1895, Rutherford came to the Cavendish Laboratory at Cambridge, in England, where he studied under J. J. Thomson. In 1898, Rutherford took a post as a professor of physics at McGill University in Montreal, Canada. He moved back to England in 1907 to work at the University of Manchester. Rutherford's most important accomplishment was his nuclear theory of atomic structure, called the Rutherford atomic model. In 1914, he was knighted for his many accomplishments. In 1919, he became head of the Cavendish Laboratory.

Major Charles Sweeney

Major Charles W. Sweeney piloted the B-29 bomber, named the Great Artiste, which dropped the atomic bomb over Nagasaki on August 9, 1945.

Leo Szilard

Leo Szilard (1898-1964) was a Hungarian physicist who was a key figure in the formation of the Manhattan Project. Szilard earned his doctoral degree from the University of Berlin in 1922. He worked as a staff member at the Institute of Theoretical Physics at the University of Berlin until

1933, when Hitler came to power, and he left Germany. Szilard worked for several years at the college of St. Bartholomew's Hospital in England, before moving to the United States to occupy a post at Colombia University. From 1942 to 1945, Szilard worked on the Manhattan Project with Fermi's research team at the University of Chicago. After the war, he accepted a position as professor of biophysics at the University of Chicago. Following the war, Szilard became a strong advocate of the use of atomic energy for peaceful purposes and supported limitations on the nuclear arms race.

Edward Teller

Edward Teller (1908-) was a Hungarian-born Jewish nuclear physicist who worked on the Manhattan Project. Teller worked with Enrico Fermi at the University of Chicago before joining the research team at Los Alamos, New Mexico. However, Teller was more interested in research into the development of a hydrogen bomb, which was considered a lesser priority during World War II. After the war, however, Teller became a leading proponent of United States efforts to create a hydrogen bomb, which was potentially more powerful than the atom bomb. In 1951, Teller collaborated with Stanislaw Ulam in a major breakthrough for research on the hydrogen bomb known as the Teller-Ulam configuration. Teller was thus dubbed the "father of the H-bomb."

Sir J. J. Thomson

J. J. Thomson (1856-1940) was an English physicist who discovered the electron in 1897. Thomson began research at the Cavendish Laboratory of Cambridge University in 1880 and in 1884 was made chair of the physics department there. For his accomplishments, Thomson was granted the Nobel Prize for physics in 1906 and was knighted in 1908. Thomson was an influential teacher at Cavendish, and many of his students, including Ernest Rutherford, were awarded Nobel Prizes.

Colonel Paul Tibbets

Colonel Paul W. Tibbets, Jr. was the pilot who flew the B-29 bomber, named Enola Gay, which dropped the atomic bomb on Hiroshima, in Japan, on August 6, 1945.

President Harry Truman

Harry S. Truman (1884-1972) was the thirty-third president of the United States. He took office on April 12, 1945, the day of President Roosevelt's death. Upon being sworn into office, Truman was apprised of the developments of the Manhattan Project, about which he had known little up to that point. While he attended the Potsdam Conference to discuss peace negotiations between the Allies and a defeated Germany, he received notice that the first atomic bomb had been successfully tested by the

Manhattan Project on July 16. From Potsdam, a message was sent to Japan, threatening the use of a devastating new weapon unless they agreed to unconditional surrender. When Japan refused this offer, Truman ordered the dropping of the atomic bomb on Hiroshima on August 6, 1945, and on Nagasaki on August 9, 1945.

H. G. Wells

H. G. Wells (1866-1946) was an English writer known today primarily for his classic science fiction novels such as *The Time Machine* (1895), *The Island of Doctor Moreau* (1896), *The Invisible Man* (1897), and *The War of the Worlds* (1898). Wells' novel *The World Set Free* (1914) was prophetic in essentially predicting atomic warfare.

Eugene Wigner

Eugene Wigner (1902-1995) was a Hungarian-born physicist who shared the 1963 Nobel Prize for physics for his work on nuclear physics. Wigner received his doctoral degree in 1925 from the Institute of Technology in Berlin. In 1938, he became a professor of mathematical physics at Princeton University, a position that he held until 1971, when he retired. In 1939, Wigner, with Leo Szilard, helped to convince Albert Einstein to draft a letter to President Roosevelt, alerting him of the possibility of developing an atomic bomb. Wigner worked with Enrico Fermi at the University of Chicago Metallurgical Laboratory, part of the

Manhattan Project.

Scientific Community

Rhodes devotes almost the entire first third of *The Making of the Atomic Bomb* to introducing the international community of scientists whose work contributed to the development of the first atomic bomb. Rhodes provides biographical background on scientists from Denmark, Germany, Italy, Austria, Hungary, Great Britain, and the United States. Even before the Manhattan Project formally brought these men and women together, many of them were either familiar with one another's work, had communicated with one another, studied with one another, or collaborated on their research. For instance, several of them worked or studied at the Cavendish Laboratory at Cambridge University in England. Further, the oppressive conditions in Germany under Hitler led many of these scientists who were Jewish to flee Nazi Germany, often settling in the United States or Britain. Rhodes explains in detail the ways in which the research, discoveries, and theoretical developments pioneered by each scientist or team of scientists drew from and added to the work of other scientists. Further, several scientists met informally in New York City and in Chicago, before the formulation of the Manhattan Project, to discuss strategies for alerting the United States government to the importance of developing an atomic bomb before Germany achieved the same end. For instance, several of them worked together at various points to draft letters to United States officials, explaining the urgency of the matter. Finally, the Manhattan Project itself, carried out simultaneously in several locations throughout the United States, represents the collaborative efforts of some of the most brilliant scientists of the twentieth century (many of whom were Nobel Prize winners in physics and chemistry).

Weapons of Mass Destruction

Rhodes is particularly concerned with the implications of nuclear warfare on the fate of the human race. Scientists working on the Manhattan Project were painfully aware of the potentially apocalyptic consequences of developing a weapon of mass destruction. Throughout their research, they debated and discussed the fate of world politics in the wake of atomic warfare. They had no doubt that the knowledge and resources to create nuclear weapons would be within the reach of many nations before long and that this could potentially result in mutual mass destruction by warring nations—the self-immolation of the human race. However, others felt convinced that, because such a universally horrific outcome could result from nuclear warfare, it might in fact be the cause of world peace. Some even believed that the potential for nuclear warfare would inevitably result in a new organization of world politics, whereby all nations would become one, and war would be completely abolished. Others were more cynical, foreseeing the horrors of implementing such a weapon. Rhodes spends considerable time quoting from interviews of victims of the bombing of Hiroshima, making vivid and visceral the effects of the bomb on human lives. He provides extensive descriptions of the aftermath of the bombing in which the charred flesh of the survivors, their skin hanging from their bodies like rags, is perhaps the most prominent image. Rhodes thus attempts to provide the reader with an idea of the deeply felt moral and ethical dilemmas of the scientists responsible for the bomb and the pure horror of the human suffering that resulted from their efforts.

Research and Sources

As a work of nonfiction, Rhodes' success in writing *The Making of the Atomic Bomb* is largely due to the thoroughness and skill with which he conducted his research. Rhodes spent five years researching and writing this history, which combines information from a variety of sources. One of his sources was classified government documents, such as the FBI files that include the record of a secret investigation of Szilard, one of the scientists on the Manhattan Project. Another source was first-person accounts by Japanese survivors of the bombing of Hiroshima, describing in graphic detail the devastation caused by the bomb. Another source was reproductions of important correspondence between scientists and politicians, such as the letter written by Einstein to the United States government, warning of the possibility of Germany building an atomic bomb. Yet another source of material Rhodes incorporates into his narrative are anecdotal accounts of private conversations between scientists involved in the Manhattan Project.

Nonfiction Genres

Drawing from a wide variety of source materials, Rhodes' narrative also combines elements of a variety of genres, or categories, of nonfiction. His book is part biography, in the sense that he provides extensive biographical background on many of the scientists whose work lead up to the making of the first atomic bomb. It is partly a political history, as Rhodes describes the political and diplomatic significance of historical events surrounding the development of the bomb. It also falls into the category of history of science, as Rhodes traces the series of scientific developments, beginning in the mid-nineteenth century, which made it possible to create an atomic bomb.

Narrative Voice

Rhodes' success with *The Making of the Atomic Bomb* can also be attributed to his capacity for encompassing a massive accumulation of data and several nonfiction genres into a single, coherent, accessible narrative. Rhodes covers a century of history, and an entire globe of political, sociological, and scientific events with a smoothly flowing, comprehensible, as well as comprehensive, third-person narrative voice.

Topics for Further Study

- Learn more about the development
  of methods for harnessing nuclear
  power as an energy source for
  peaceful purposes. What scientific
  research resulted in the construction
  of nuclear power plants? When was
  the first nuclear power plant
  constructed? What types of
  opposition arose to the development
  of nuclear power plants? What is the
  status of nuclear energy as a
  peacetime power source in the
  United States today? What about in
  other nations?

- The research of many scientists
  throughout the first half of the
  twentieth century led up to the
  realization that an atomic bomb was

possible. Pick one of these scientists from the Key Figures list in this entry, and learn more about his or her research up to 1942 when the Manhattan Project was organized. How did this scientist's research contribute to the creation of the first atomic bomb?

- Learn more about the impact of the atomic bomb on Japan. How did the Japanese government and people respond to the horrors of Hiroshima and Nagasaki in the post-war years?

- What is the status of nuclear weapons in the world today? To what extent does nuclear warfare continue to be a threat to the populations of the world?

Epigraphs

Rhodes makes use of epigraphs—short, pithy quotations—at the beginning of each of the three parts of the book and facing the table of contents. The very first of these quotes is by Robert Oppenheimer, director of the Los Alamos, New Mexico, branch of the Manhattan Project; it reads: "Taken as a story of human achievement, and human blindness, the discoveries in the sciences are among the great epics." Such a reference to mythological or biblical tales of human heroism and folly is entirely apt as an opening to Rhodes' arguably "epic" nine-hundred page history of the atomic bomb. This quote captures Rhodes' attitude toward the development of the first nuclear weapon, as both a monument to scientific "achievement," and as a testament to a certain moral "blindness" to the horrors that were to result from this achievement. A second opening quote is from Emilio Segré. In this comment, Segré emphasizes a certain element of luck in the various political and scientific efforts that went into the making of the bomb. In offering this quote, Rhodes indirectly comments upon the extent to which minute facts of physical reality—"solid numbers based on measurement"—can potentially determine the fate of human history.

World War II

World War II was waged between the Allied forces and the Axis forces in the years 1939 to 1945. The first use of the atomic bomb was instrumental in determining the outcome of the war.

World War II began on August 31, 1939, when Germany, under Adolph Hitler, invaded Poland. As a result, Great Britain and France declared war on Germany on September 3. Soviet troops invaded Poland's eastern border on September 17, and Germany and the Soviet Union agreed to divide a defeated Poland between them. By October 10, Soviet forces easily established themselves in Estonia, Latvia, and Lithuania. Meanwhile, skirmishes between British naval forces and German U-boats (submarines) took place in September and October of that year.

In February 1940, the Soviet Union attacked Finland, achieving victory by March 6. In April, Germany successfully invaded and occupied both Denmark and Norway. In May, Germany successfully invaded and occupied Belgium. From there, German troops invaded northern France, beating back French and British troops. On June 10, Italy, under Mussolini, aligned itself with Germany by declaring war on France and Great Britain. The French government surrendered to both Germany and Italy, agreeing to a partitioning of France into an occupied zone and an unoccupied zone. In July, the occupied French government, known as the Vichy, consented to the creation of a new French nation under German rule. Accordingly, France ended its alliance with Great Britain against Germany.

Having broken the French-British alliance, Germany began attacks on British air and naval forces in an extended conflict known as the Battle of Britain. When German bombing attacks moved further into British territory, Great Britain retaliated by bombing Berlin. Hitler responded to this offensive with the bombing of London and other British cities. Germany continued air raids over Great Britain into April 1941; however, the British ultimately held off a German invasion with Britain's superior radar technology that allowed them to detect and shoot down many German planes.

In October 1940, Italy began a war against Greece. In April and May 1941, Germany successfully invaded and occupied both Yugoslavia and Greece. As a result, Yugoslavia was broken into several separate states, and Greece was divided between German and Italian occupation zones. On June 22, 1941, German troops invaded Russia.

Up to this point, the United States had remained officially neutral with regard to the war. However, on December 7, 1941, Japanese forces bombed the United States naval base at Pearl Harbor in a surprise attack. As a result, on December 8, the United States declared war on

Japan. Japan had invaded China in the years previous to World War II, and, immediately after the United States declared war on Japan, China declared war on Italy, Germany, and Japan. On April 18, 1942, the United States bombed Tokyo in an air raid using conventional explosives. With the United States at war, preparations for the secret Manhattan Project to develop the first atomic bomb were made by United States government and military officials.

In January 1943, Roosevelt and Churchill met at the Casablanca Conference, as a result of which Roosevelt announced a request for the unconditional surrender of Germany, Italy, and Japan. On July 25 of that year, Mussolini resigned his rule in Italy, after which the new Italian government secretly negotiated with the Allies. In August, the Allies took Sicily. In September, the Allies landed in Italy, which soon surrendered. On October 13, Italy, now aligned with the Allies, declared war on Germany.

The decisive event of the war was the invasion of German occupied Normandy by American, British, and Canadian troops on June 6, 1944, known as D day. When, in April 1945, Allied troops made their way into Germany and surrounded Berlin, Hitler committed suicide. On May 8, 1945, Germany officially surrendered to the Allies.

Meanwhile, war continued on the Pacific front between the Allies and Japan. The Potsdam Conference, in which the leaders of the Allied forces met in a suburb outside Berlin, was held from

July 17 to August 2, 1945. During this time, Truman was notified of the successful testing of the first atomic bomb, named Trinity, by members of the Manhattan Project. At this point, Stalin was informed of the United States' possession of an atomic bomb. The Allies had made much progress in defeating Japanese forces in the Pacific theater of war, and, on July 26, a declaration was sent from Potsdam to Japan, calling for unconditional surrender and warning of reprisals if this demand was not met.

Compare & Contrast

- **1949:** The North Atlantic Treaty Organization is founded to create an alliance between the United States and nations of Western Europe in opposition to the military might of the Soviet Union in much of Eastern Europe.

- **1955:** The Warsaw Pact forms a military alliance between the Soviet Union and other Eastern European nations.

- **1963:** The Nuclear Test Ban Treaty, signed by the United States, the Soviet Union, and the United Kingdom, bans the testing of nuclear weapons in the earth's atmosphere, in outer space, and underwater; it limits the testing of atomic weapons to underground sites.

- **1967:** The Outer Space Treaty is signed by the United States, the Soviet Union, the United Kingdom, and other nations; it declares that space exploration be conducted for peaceful purposes only and that no nation may claim sovereignty over the moon or any other region of outer space.

- **1968:** The Nuclear Non-Proliferation Treaty, signed by the United States, the Soviet Union, the United Kingdom, and many other nations, claims that no nation shall aid another nation that does not possess a nuclear arsenal in the development or build up of nuclear weapons.

- **1987:** The Intermediate Range Nuclear Forces (INF) Treaty is signed between the United States and the Soviet Union, resulting in the dismantling of some 2,600 missiles and granting each side the right to verify and inspect compliance with the terms of the treaty. This is the first treaty to completely dismantle a particular category of nuclear weapons system.

- **1945:** Over the next forty-five years, the buildup of nuclear arms in the context of the Cold War between the United States and the Soviet Union results in an arms race with the potential to result in mutual mass-destruction.

- **1947:** The term Cold War is first used to characterize the chilly status of international relations between the United States and the Soviet Union.

- **1962:** During the Cuban Missile Crisis, the United States learns that the Soviets have installed nuclear missiles in Cuba. In the course of a diplomatic standoff between President John F. Kennedy and Soviet Premier Nikita Khrushchev, both sides are on the brink of initiating global nuclear warfare. However, Khrushchev backs down, agreeing to remove all nuclear weapons from Cuba in exchange for a United States promise never to invade Cuba.

- **1972:** The Strategic Arms Limitations Talks (SALT), held between the United States and the Soviet Union, result in the signing of the Anti-Ballistic Missile Treaty (ABM). The ABM Treaty places limitations on the build up of weapons designed to destroy incoming nuclear weapons.

- **1979:** SALT II negotiations result in the proposal of a treaty to limit nuclear weapons, but neither side signs the treaty. However, both sides subsequently adhere to the limitations set by the treaty.

- **1983:** President Ronald Reagan announces his proposal for the development of a Strategic Defense Initiative (SDI), which would include the build up of nuclear weaponry in outer space. However, the "Star Wars" initiative remains controversial throughout the 1980s and is essentially abandoned with the break up of the Soviet Union from 1989-1991.

- **1989-1991:** The collapse of the Soviet Union into fifteen independent, sovereign nations effectively ends the Cold War.

- **1991-1992:** The Strategic Arms Reduction Talks (START) between the United States and the Soviet Union resume the SALT I and SALT II negotiations. With the collapse of the Soviet Union and effective end of the Cold War, both sides agree to significant reduction (of 10-15 percent) in their nuclear arsenal by the dismantling of many existing weapons.

As Japan refused to surrender, the United States dropped an atomic bomb on the city of Hiroshima on August 6. Japanese government authorities did not entirely comprehend the degree of devastation caused by the new weapon and did not surrender until a second atomic bomb was dropped on the city of Nagasaki on August 9. On August 10, Japan communicated its acceptance of an unconditional surrender, officially surrendering to the Allies on August 14. On September 9, Japan formalized their surrender to China, thus ending World War II.

Critical Overview

Upon publication, *The Making of the Atomic Bomb* enjoyed both critical acclaim and popular success. Rhodes was rewarded for his years of meticulous research when he won the 1987 National Book Award, the 1988 Pulitzer Prize for General Nonfiction, and the 1988 National Book Critics Circle Award for General Nonfiction.

Critics praise Rhodes for his exhaustive research, comprehensive scope, even-handed reportage, and narrative skills in rendering a nearly overwhelming array of historical information into a dramatic story, successfully integrating clear explanation of complex scientific concepts with a humanizing account of the scientists, military officials, and political figures involved in the Manhattan Project.

Solly Zuckerman, in a 1988 review in the *New Republic,* calls it "a monumental study," and, echoing the widespread praise Rhodes received, asserts:

> Rhodes' book richly deserves the acclaim that it has already been accorded. He has taken infinite trouble to understand and to outline in simple language the principles of nuclear physics that are the foundation on which the story of the bomb rests. The personalities who

move through his book come to life in a way that they are unlikely to have done had they been depicted by a scientist's pen.

Zuckerman further observes, "I have no doubt that his book will stand for years to come as an authoritative account of the way our nuclear age started," adding, "Above all, lengthy as it is, it will be enjoyed as a magnificent read."

In addition to his narrative skills, Rhodes is praised for his balanced treatment of controversial subject matter. David Bennett, in *Dictionary of Literary Biography,* notes that *The Making of the Atomic Bomb* "draws much of its strength and vigor from Rhodes' reporting prowess." He observes, "Despite his own feelings about the subject, Rhodes largely remains a dispassionate narrator, an objective historian, never taking sides on the nuclear debate, giving equal space to myriad points of view."

Rhodes' sequel to *The Making of the Atomic Bomb*, entitled *Dark Sun: The Making of the Hydrogen Bomb* (1995), was named one of the best books of 1995 by *Publishers Weekly.* Critical response to *Dark Sun* expresses praise for Rhodes on similar grounds to that of the earlier book. Richard Stengel, in a review in *Time* magazine, calls it "epic and fascinating." A review in *The Economist* states, "Readers of Mr. Rhodes's magnificent *The Making of the Atomic Bomb*... could not wish for a better chronicler for the subsequent installment. The insight, learning and narrative skill displayed in that first volume are gathered here again." A reviewer in *Publishers Weekly* expresses the response of many critics to both books by stating, "Rhodes makes history work as drama."

In addition to *The Making of the Atomic Bomb* and *Dark Sun*, Rhodes has written a wide variety of fiction and nonfiction books that demonstrate the broad scope of his research and writing abilities. In 1973, he published *The Ungodly*, a well-researched fictionalized narrative of the Donner Party, a group of Pioneers who, stranded in the mountains by a snowstorm, resorted to cannibalism to survive. *Farm: A Year in the Life of an American Farmer* (1989), was the culmination of a year spent researching the daily activities and financial struggles of a family of farmers. *A Hole in the World: An American Boyhood* (1990) is Rhodes' autobiographical account of the abuse he and his brother experienced as boys. *Nuclear Renewal* (1993) argues for the expanded use of nuclear power plants, which has come to be largely discounted as an unviable energy source. In *How to Write: Advice and Reflections* (1995), Rhodes offers advice to aspiring writers, based on his own experience. *Trying to Get Some Dignity: Stories of Childhood Abuse* (1996), written with third wife Ginger Rhodes, is based on interview material with survivors of childhood abuse.

What Do I Read Next?

- *Farm: A Year in the Life of an American Farmer* (1989), by Richard Rhodes, is based on the year Rhodes spent chronicling the daily activities and financial struggles of a Missouri farm family.

- *A Hole in the World: An American Boyhood* (1990), by Richard Rhodes, is Rhodes' autobiographical account of the years of abuse he and his brother suffered at the hands of their stepmother.

- *Dark Sun: The Making of the Hydrogen Bomb* (1995), by Richard Rhodes, is Rhodes' celebrated sequel to *The Making of the Atomic Bomb*, in which he chronicles the research leading to the development of the first hydrogen bomb.

- *Picturing the Bomb: Photographs from the Secret World of the Manhattan Project* (1995), by Rachel Fermi and Esther Samra, is a photographic account of the research and testing done by the Manhattan Project during the development of the first atomic bomb.

- *Hiroshima: Why America Dropped the Atomic Bomb* (1995), by Ronald Takaki, is an analysis of the social, political, and historical context of the American decision to drop the first atomic bomb on Hiroshima, Japan.

- *Weapons for Victory: The Hiroshima Decision Fifty Years Later* (1995), by Robert James Maddox, provides a discussion of the impact of the dropping of the first atomic bomb, in 1945, on politics and international relations in the late twentieth century. This book also offers a discussion of the moral and ethical issues raised by the United States decision to drop the bomb on Hiroshima.

Sources

Bennett, David, *Dictionary of Literary Biography, Volume 185: American Literary Journalists, 1945-1995, First Series,* Gale Research, 1997, pp. 241-252.

Hershberg, James G., and James B. Conant, *Harvard to Hiroshima and the Making of the Nuclear Age,* Stanford University Press, 1993.

Review in *The Economist,* Vol. 337, No. 7935, October 7, 1995, p. 99.

Review in *Publishers Weekly,* Vol. 242, No. 40, October 2, 1995, p. 40.

Rhodes, Richard, *The Making of the Atomic Bomb,* Simon and Schuster, 1986

Stengel, Richard, Review in *Time,* Vol. 146, No. 8, August 21, 1995, p. 66.

Zuckerman, Solly, Review in *The New Republic,* Vol. 199, No. 8, August 22, 1988, p. 38.

Further Reading

Allen, Thomas B., and Norman Polmar, *Code-Name Downfall: The Secret Plan to Invade Japan and Why Truman Dropped the Bomb,* Simon & Schuster, 1995.

> Allen and Polmar discuss United States military strategy in respect to President Truman's decision to drop the atomic bomb on Hiroshima.

Alperovitz, Gar, *The Decision to Use the Atomic Bomb and the Architecture of an American Myth,* Knopf, 1995.

> Alperovitz presents a critical historical perspective on the United States military strategy and international relations with the Allied nations during World War II in respect to the dropping of the atomic bomb on Hiroshima.

Larsen, Rebecca, *Oppenheimer and the Atomic Bomb,* F. Watts, 1988.

> Larsen provides a biography of Robert J. Oppenheimer, a leading scientist in the Manhattan Project, which developed the first atomic bomb.

Lifton, Robert Jay, and Greg Mitchell, *Hiroshima in America: Fifty Years of Denial,* Putnam, 1995.

Lifton and Mitchell discuss the moral and ethical implications of the ways in which the bombing of Hiroshima has been represented in American history.

Rhodes, Richard, *Deadly Feasts: Tracking the Secrets of a Terrifying New Plague*, Simon & Schuster, 1997.

Rhodes discusses the potential threat to humans from a category of infectious diseases known as "mad cow disease" in its bovine form.

———, *How to Write: Advice and Reflections*, Morrow, 1995.

Rhodes offers advice to the aspiring writer, based on his personal experience as a journalist, novelist, and nonfiction writer.

———, ed., *Visions of Technology: A Century of Vital Debate About Machines, Systems, and the Human World*, Simon & Schuster, 1999.

Visions of Technology provides a collection of articles that address the social, historical, and ethical impact of various technological developments throughout the twentieth century.

Rhodes, Richard, and Ginger Rhodes, *Trying to Get Some Dignity: Stories of Triumph Over Childhood Abuse*, W. Morrow, 1996.

Rhodes and Rhodes compiled *Trying to Get Some Dignity* using interviews with adult survivors of childhood abuse.

Printed in the USA
CPSIA information can be obtained
at www.ICGtesting.com
LVHW012050110823
754959LV00004B/368